DANGEROUS JOBS

UNDERWATER CONSTRUCTION WORKERS

CLARA CELLA

Lerner Publications ◆ Minneapolis

Lerner Publications Company
An imprint of Lerner Publishing Group, Inc.
241 First Avenue North
Minneapolis, MN 55401 USA

For reading levels and more information, look up this title at www.lernerbooks.com.

Main body text set in ITC Franklin Gothic Std.
Typeface provided by Adobe Systems.

Library of Congress Cataloging-in-Publication Data

Names: Cella, Clara, author.
Title: Underwater construction workers / Clara Cella.
Description: Minneapolis : Lerner Publications, [2023] | Series: Updog books. Dangerous jobs | Includes bibliographical references and index. | Audience: Ages 8–11 | Audience: Grades 4–6 | Summary: "If you think construction workers have a tough job, try doing it underwater. Dive in to explore the history of underwater construction workers, the tools they use, and the dangers they face under the surface"— Provided by publisher.
Identifiers: LCCN 2022017614 (print) | LCCN 2022017615 (ebook) | ISBN 9781728475585 (lib. bdg.) | ISBN 9781728486253 (pbk.) | ISBN 9781728482026 (eb pdf)
Subjects: LCSH: Underwater construction—Juvenile literature. | Construction workers—Juvenile literature.
Classification: LCC TC195 .C45 2023 (print) | LCC TC195 (ebook) | DDC 627/.702—dc23/eng/20220623

LC record available at https://lccn.loc.gov/2022017614
LC ebook record available at https://lccn.loc.gov/2022017615

Manufactured in the United States of America
1 – CG – 12/15/22

Table of Contents

BELOW THE SURFACE

The underwater construction worker tightens a bolt. Something brushes against him. A shark? He can't tell in the dark water.

Underwater construction workers build and fix things.

They do the same tasks that workers on land do. But they do them in water.

Underwater construction workers are skilled divers. But they can get hurt.

Workers may rise from deep water too quickly and get sick.

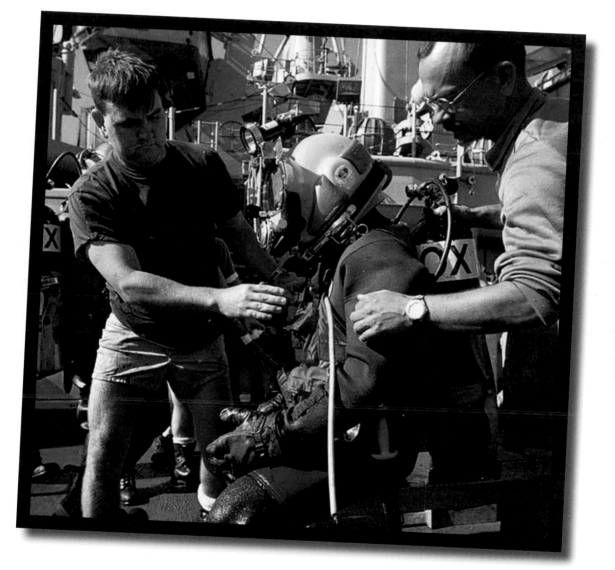

UP NEXT! DEEP BREATH.

WATER WORK

In the 1500s, underwater construction workers used diving bells. The bell fit over a worker's upper body and was filled with air. Workers could breathe underwater for only a short time.

GEAR CLOSE-UP

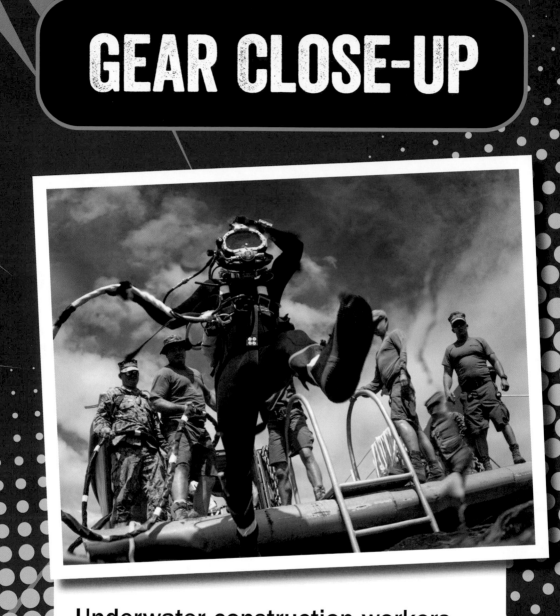

Underwater construction workers wear special gear to keep them safe.

UNDERWATER CONSTRUCTION WORKER

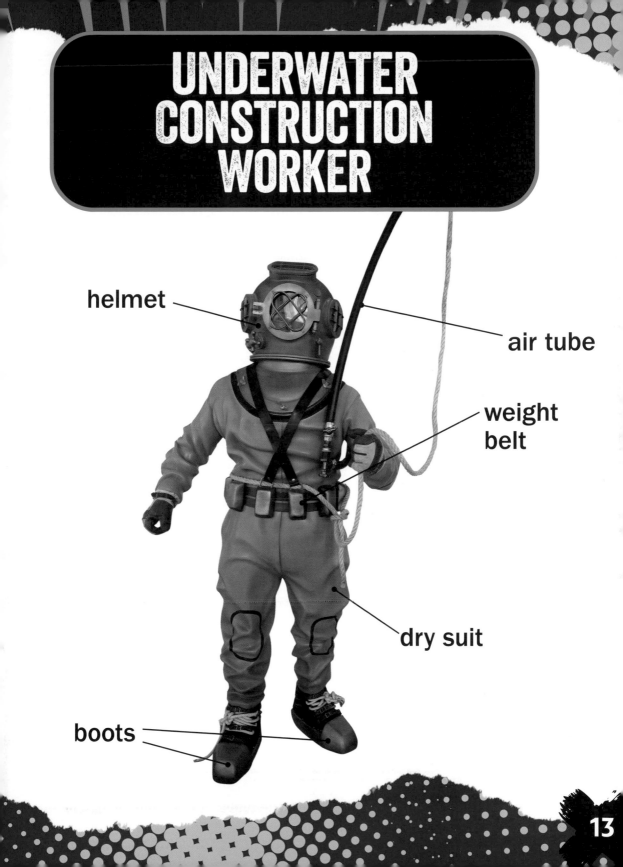

helmet

air tube

weight belt

dry suit

boots

Modern underwater construction workers work up to eight hours at a time.

modern: of the present time

They use power tools on bridges, ships, and oil rigs.

oil rig: a structure used to drill for and remove liquid fuel from the ground

UP NEXT! TEAMWORK.

DIVE IN, BE SAFE

Underwater construction workers have teams that keep them safe.

These people control the air
supply. They watch for danger
and give support.

As the world population grows, land space fills up.

population: the total number of people living in an area

Construction workers may be needed to build floating or underwater cities.

Underwater construction workers have tough but important jobs.

MEET AN UNDERWATER CONSTRUCTION WORKER

Singapore

NAME: Siti Naqiah Tusliman

BACKGROUND: Tusliman began diving for fun as a child. She later trained to clean ships underwater.

CLAIM TO FAME: In 2017, Tusliman became Singapore's first female professional diver. She does underwater construction work in a business that is mostly male.

Glossary

modern: of the present time

oil rig: a structure used to drill for and remove liquid fuel from the ground

population: the total number of people living in an area

Check It Out!

Bowman, Chris. *Construction Workers*. Minneapolis: Bellwether Media, 2018.

Britannica Kids: Underwater Diving
https://kids.britannica.com/students/article/underwater
-diving/274022

Easy Science for Kids: Channel Tunnel
https://easyscienceforkids.com/channel-tunnel/

Kiddle: Underwater Diving Facts for Kids
https://kids.kiddle.co/Underwater_diving

Spanier, Kristine. *Golden Gate Bridge*. Minneapolis: Jump!, 2022.

Index

Photo Acknowledgements

Image credits: Stocktrek Images/Getty Images, p.4; U.S. Navy/ ZUMA Press/Newscom, p.5; Lt.j.g. Joshua Jepsen/DVIDS, p.6; PH3 Salcido/U.S. National Archives, p.7; U.S. Navy/Sipa USA/ Newscom, p.8; U.S. Navy/Getty Images, p.9; George Arents Collection/New York Public Library, p.10; Saibo/Wikimedia, p.11; Petty Officer 2nd Class Sean Furey/DVIDS, p.12; arogant/ Shutterstock, p.13; Petty Officer 1st Class Michael Tuck/DVIDS, p.14; Petty Officer 1st Class Arthurgwain Marquez/DVIDS, p.15; Petty Officer 1st Class Charles/UPI/Newscom, p.16; Petty Officer 2nd Class Ryan Chatman/DVIDS, p.17; Grant Faint/ Getty Images, p.18; Daniel Bosma/Getty Images, p.19; Annette Riedl/dpa/picture-alliance/Newscom, p.20; Martin Puddy/Getty Images, p.21; Mega Pixel/Shutterstock, p.21

Design element: Infostocker/Getty Images

Cover: U.S. Navy/ZUMA Press/Newscom